At the heart
of friendship

Edited by Olivia Cytrynowicz

**Andrews McMeel
Publishing, LLC**
Kansas City

At the heart *of* friendship

07 08 09 10 11 LEO 10 9 8 7 6 5 4 3 2 1

ISBN-13: 978-0-7407-6854-5

ISBN-10: 0-7407-6854-9

Library of Congress Control Number: 2007900846
www.andrewsmcmeel.com

Design by Kelda Jackson

Contributing writers and editors: Ellen Brenneman, Dorothy Colgan, Debra Crowe, Renee Duvall, Linda Elrod, Bill Gray, Cheryl Hawkinson, Barbara Loots, Jane-Elyse Pryor, Linda Staten, Alarie Tennille, Dean Walley

At the heart
of friendship

It's

wonderful

to have someone

whom you grow to love

for being such a great person

and such a good friend.

A wonderful friend is a beautiful blend of caring and sharing and love.

*At
the very
heart of friendship
there is love.*

A
good friendship is
constantly changing and growing.
Depend on its beauty to delight you
and its strength to sustain you
through every season
of your life.

❧

*There
are moments
when a special friend
makes a difference
that no one
else can
make.*

❧

A friend
is one who creates
a circle of belonging, a sacred
space in which all is safe, all is calm,
all is good.

*One
of the secrets
of life is keeping your
friends within hugging distance.*

*There
are not many things
in life as beautiful as true friendship,
and there are not many things more
uncommon.*

Sharing
laughter, sharing tears,
sharing triumphs, sharing fears,
growing closer through the years . . .
true friendship is
forever.

❧

A
real friend
listens with her heart
and never stops believing in you
even if you give up on
yourself.

❧

Friendship
is a rainbow
between two
hearts.

A friend
is that special
someone with whom
you always feel
at ease.

MAY FRIENDS
BE TRUE

❦

*One
of the most
beautiful qualities
of true friendship is to understand
and be understood.*

❦

Friendship is a sheltering tree.

✀

Time endears and cannot fade the memories that love has made.

*Once
in a while
you will find a friend
who will be
a friend
forever.*

A true
friendship is
as wise as it is tender.

Friendship
weaves beautiful
patterns.

*A friend
can make anything
better simply
by being
there.*

The very best "remember whens" are made by very special friends.

I like
to think that we are
sent special friends to share our lives,
very special friends
we can be ourselves with,
talk with, laugh with, hope with . . .
special friends
like you.

＆

When
the news is all bad
and the sky is all gray
and the chocolate is all gone,
it's good to remember
I've got a friend
like you.

＆

Nothing on earth is more comforting than a true friendship.

*A friend
understands the
unspoken thoughts in
your heart.*

*A friend
is someone who
sees you as you wish you were
and likes you as you
really are.*

✃

People
don't talk
much about the love
friends have for one another.

We talk
about liking friends,
but some friends add so much
to our lives that "like"
just isn't strong
enough.

✃

What a
beautiful difference
your friendship has made.